CHILDREN'S
BIBLE
CLASSICS

JOSHUA AND THE BATTLE OF JERICHO

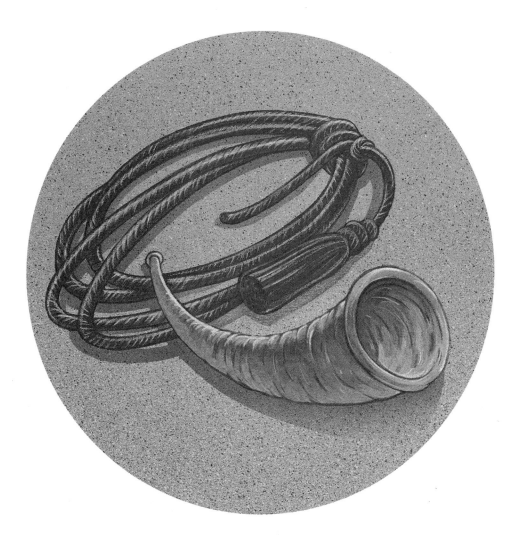

NR

NELSON REGENCY
A Division of Thomas Nelson, Inc.

First published in 1994 by
Thomas Nelson Publishers, Nashville, Tennessee.

Copyright © 1994 Bluewood Books

Story retold by Bill Yenne

Art and design direction by Bill Yenne. Illustrated by Mark
Busacca, Edwin Esquivel, Emi Fukawa, Victor Lee, Doug
Scott, Vadim Vahrameev, Hanako Wakiyama, and Bill Yenne.
Special thanks to Ruth DeJauregui.

Produced by
Bluewood Books (A Division of The Siyeh Group, Inc.)
P.O. Box 460313, San Francisco, CA 94146

Yenne, Bill, 1949-
    Joshua and the Battle of Jericho/[story retold for this
edition by Bill Yenne].
    p.   cm.—(Children's Bible Classics)
    ISBN 0-7852-8327-7 (MM).—ISBN 0-7852-8331-5 (TR)
    1. Joshua (Biblical figure)—Juvenile literature.   2. Bible
stories, English—O.T. Joshua [1. Joshua (Biblical figure)
2. Bible Stories—O.T.] I. Title. II. Series.
BS580.J7Y46 1994
222'.109505—dc20   93-35873
                                                        CIP
                                                        AC

94 95 96 97 98—1 2 3 4 5

Printed and bound in the United States of America

JOSHUA AND THE BATTLE OF JERICHO

After the time of Moses, the children of Israel were still camped upon the east bank of the river Jordan. God spoke to Joshua, saying, "Now that Moses is gone, you are to take his place. Lead the people across the river Jordan to the land which I have promised to them. Be strong and brave. I will be with you as I was with Moses."

Joshua gave orders to his officers, saying, "Go through the camp and tell the people to prepare food for a journey. In three days we will cross the river Jordan and go into the Promised Land as the Lord has told us."

Then Joshua chose two brave and strong young men. He told them to go as spies across the river and look at the city of Jericho. Before the rest of the land could be claimed, the Israelites would have to capture this city. Joshua told the men to find out all they could about the land.

The two men did as Joshua said and went to Jericho.
But they were spotted by the enemy, and the king of
Jericho sent men to capture them.

The two spies hurried to a house near the wall of the city. The house belonged to a woman named Rahab. She hid the men on the roof of her house and covered them with plant stalks so they could not be seen. The soldiers could not find the spies so they went away thinking that the spies had escaped.

Rahab said, "All of us in this city know that your God is mighty and that He has given you this land. When you capture this city, please promise me that you will spare my life and the lives of my family."

The two men said, "We promise that no harm will come to you, for you have saved our lives."

Rahab let a rope down outside the window of her house so the men could slide down to the ground. They said to Rahab, "When our men come, hang the scarlet cord in the window. We will tell them not to harm the people in the house where they see the scarlet cord."

The two men hid on the
mountain for three days. Then
they told their story to
Joshua.

"It is true the Lord has
given us all the land," they
said. "The people are afraid
of us."

Joshua commanded the people to move their camp. When Joshua gave the word, they marched toward the river Jordan. They stayed there for three days.

Then Joshua said, "Let the priests carry the Ark of the Covenant with the Ten Commandments in front, and let there be a space between it and the rest of the people. Do not come near the Ark."

Joshua said to the priests, "Now walk into the water of the river."

Then a most wonderful thing happened. As soon as the feet of the priests touched the water by the shore, the river

stopped flowing. This left a dry path to go across! The priests carried the Ark down to the middle of the dry river bed.

Joshua gave the order to march across. As the people passed through, the priests stayed in the middle of the river bed, holding the Ark.

Then Joshua called for one man from each of the twelve tribes. He told them to gather twelve stones from the river and build a memorial on the river bed.

When the priests who carried the Ark left the river bed, the river once again began to flow. Now that the children of Israel had reached the land that God had promised to their fathers, they set up a new camp. They built a memorial there just like the one on the river bed.

It was the time of the early harvest, and in the fields they found grain. They gathered it and made bread.

Near the new camp stood the mighty walls of Jericho. When Joshua went out to look at the city, he saw a man holding a sword in front of him. Joshua bravely said to him, "Are you on our side or are you one of our enemies?"

The man said, "Neither. I am the commander of the army of the Lord."

Joshua fell down to the ground and worshipped him.
"What does my Lord want me to do?" Joshua asked.
The commander of God's army replied, "Take off your
sandals. You are standing on holy ground."

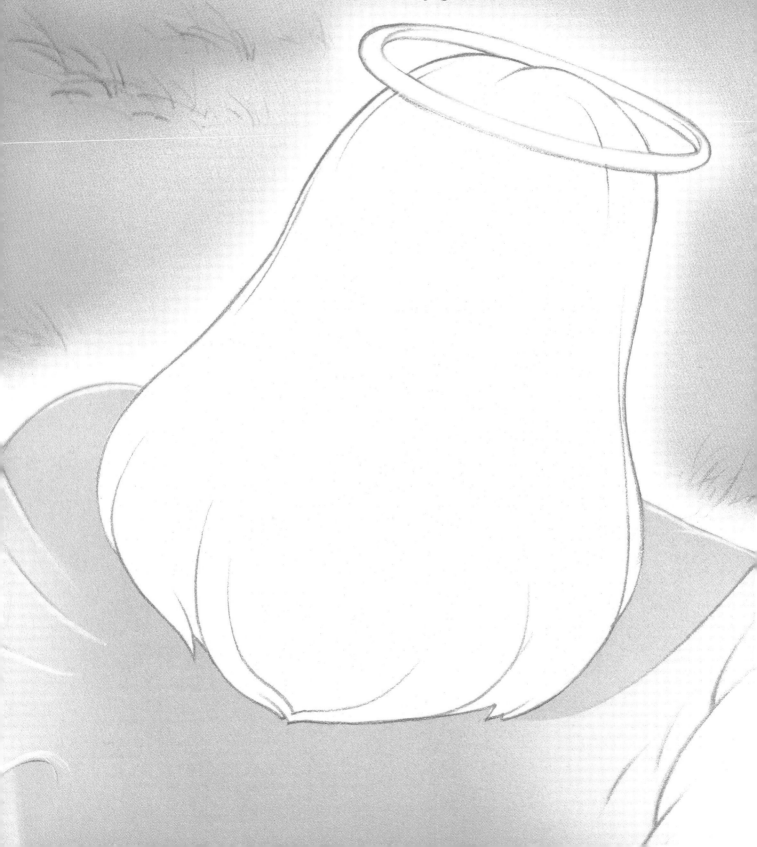

The Lord's commander told Joshua, "I have given the city of Jericho to you."

Then he gave Joshua instructions on how to capture the city.

Joshua went back to the camp and got the people ready to march around the city as God had told him.
In front came the soldiers and next came the priests carrying trumpets made of rams' horns. They blew these long and loud.

Next came the Ark of the Covenant, held on the shoulders of the priests. Last of all came the people of Israel. The only sound was the rams' horn trumpets as they marched around the walls of Jericho. Joshua had commanded the people not to make a sound until he gave the order.

Again the next morning they marched around the walls of the city. They did this each day for six days. On the seventh day, by God's command, they got up very early in the morning. They did not stop when they had marched around the walls once. They kept on marching around and around until they had circled the city seven times.

The seventh time they marched around the city, the priests blew the trumpets. Joshua then said, "Shout! For the Lord has given you the city!"

Then a great shout went up from the people. Everyone looked at the wall and saw it shake and fall with a great crash!

Joshua said to the two brave spies, "Go and bring out Rahab and her family and take them to a safe place."

The two men went into Rahab's house and brought her out with her father and mother and all her family. They cared for them and kept them safely in the camp of the Israelites.

Joshua told the Israelites, "Nothing in this city belongs to you. It is the Lord's and it will be destroyed as an offering to the Lord."

They gathered up all the gold and silver and precious things, and all that was in the houses. They took nothing for themselves, but kept the gold and silver and the things made of brass and iron for the house of the Lord. The rest was burned as Joshua instructed.